Contents

SAY WHAT?

What you have in front of you is a genuine book of original tongue twisters. Very well, you say, what should I do with this book? Is it a doorstop, a bedtime story, a quiet book to read alone?

No and no and no! And, possibly, no again. This is a book to be read aloud! Think about it.

Tongue twisters are for twisting your tongue around. For saying three times fast! For making your friends look, well, ridiculous! That's what this book is for. For making the root beer come out your nose or, better yet, the nose of your friends.

But best of all, tongue twisters are for inventing. Once you've read some of the ones in this book, make some up yourself.

Test them out on those parents of yours. Make them beg for mercy. Tie their tongues in knots. In fact, they'll probably have some good tongue twisters of their own for you. About dinosaurs and when the earth was young.

Keep this in mind though. When you make people sputter their way through a tongue twister from this book or one of your own making, they will be slurring and stammering and looking goofy. So get ready to be covered in spit and to try your own tongue at ones that they make up.

You have been warned.

Have a ridiculously good time with what comes next!

Christopher A. Tait
Professor, Tonguetwisticus

Quick and Tricky

Tongue twisters to begin with

All right, now, let's start off with some tongue
twisters that will get you limbered up. Now,
don't do yourself an injury. The trick here is to
start off nice and slow. We'll get complicated
later. The challenge is as old as time and,
possibly, your parents.

She Says

She says she saw it.
She says she saw it.
She says she saw it.

She Should Say

She should say she's sorry.
She should say she's sorry.
She should say she's sorry.

She Sneezes

She sneezes, sways, and snores and swoons.
She sneezes, sways, and snores and swoons.
She sneezes, sways, and snores and swoons.

Sheer Drivel

Drivel, dribble,
  quibble, spittle.
    Drivel, dribble,
      quibble, spittle.
        Drivel, dribble,
          quibble, spittle.

Thick as Thieves

Thick as three tricky thieves.
Thick as three tricky thieves.
Thick as three tricky thieves.

The Three Thieves Leave

They've seen three thieves leave the scene!
They've seen three thieves leave the scene!
They've seen three thieves leave the scene!

Slither Hither

Slither hither through the slick thistled
thickets.
Slither hither through the slick thistled
thickets.
Slither hither through the slick thistled
thickets.

Nine Knitting Nannies

Nine nannies needed new knitting needles
   nightly, for the knitting needing mending.
Nine nannies needed new knitting needles
   nightly, for the knitting needing mending.
Nine nannies needed new knitting needles
   nightly, for the knitting needing mending.

Foxtrots

Foxtrots tie feet in knots.
Foxtrots tie feet in knots.
Foxtrots tie feet in knots.

A Great Day

A great, gray, grade A day.
A great, gray, grade A day.
A great, gray, grade A day.

Is It Better?

Is it better being bitter or
  better being brighter?
Is it better being bitter or
  better being brighter?
Is it better being bitter or
  better being brighter?

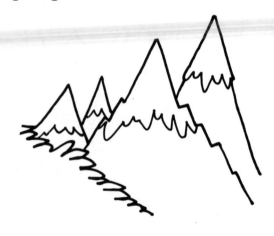

A Copper Key

A copper key, cut properly,
  keeps care of costly property!
A copper key, cut properly,
  keeps care of costly property!
A copper key, cut properly,
  keeps care of costly property!

One Smoke

Just one smoke will choke a yodeler
  before he croaks a single yodel!

Six Slick Sticks

Six slick sticks on a sticky stretch of street.
Six slick sticks on a sticky stretch of street.
Six slick sticks on a sticky stretch of street.

Pointy Pencil Points

Pointy pencil points poke at pulpy paper pads.
Pointy pencil points poke at pulpy paper pads.
Pointy pencil points poke at pulpy paper pads.

That Brick

That brick broke the back
  of the bloke who built that
    black brick building!

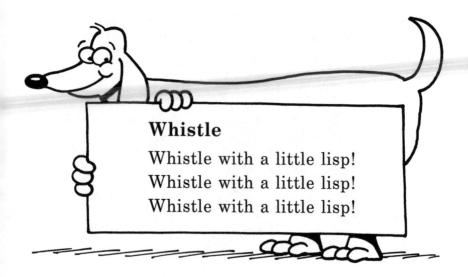

Whistle

Whistle with a little lisp!
Whistle with a little lisp!
Whistle with a little lisp!

He Brought Her Back

I'll bet he brought her back because he brought
  her back the pack he bought!
I'll bet he brought her back because he brought
  her back the pack he bought!
I'll bet he brought her back because he brought
  her back the pack he bought!

Pop a Tin

Pop a tin or trim a pop.
Pop a tin or trim a pop.
Pop a tin or trim a pop.

Arithma-trick

Ninety-nine
and ninety-nine
added is
twice times
ninety-nine!

Where Bears Be There, Beware!

Tongue twisters from the wild

This is where things get hairy. And fuzzy. And even a little feathery at times. Tongue twisters from the animal kingdom. They're hard to say and they have no manners. What, were they raised in a barn? Go ahead, get in there and make some silly squawking noises!

Wedded Wildlife

Why wouldn't wedded woodland wildlife wear
  wooden wedding rings?
Why wouldn't wedded woodland wildlife wear
  wooden wedding rings?
Why wouldn't wedded woodland wildlife wear
  wooden wedding rings?

To Pinch a Finch

To pinch a finch you clinch a sack
And cinch behind the finch's back
And inching to the finch's nest
You cinch the sack and pinch the rest.

Bored Boars

Bored boars, busy boars.
Bored boars, busy boars.
Bored boars, busy boars.

Could a Barracuda?

Could a barracuda cut a can of buttered beans?
Could a barracuda cut a can of buttered beans?
Could a barracuda cut a can of buttered beans?

Baaad Haircut

Sheep should
  seem clean
  so sheer your sheep
  so that it's shaved and shorn.

Smell the Smelt

Smell that smelly summer smelt.
Smell that smelly summer smelt.
Smell that smelly summer smelt.

Cramming Clams

You can cram clams in cans if you can,
But you can't clam up a Scottish clan.

We Walruses

We walruses won't wear winter
   wool in warm weather.
     We walruses won't wear winter
        wool in warm weather.
          We walruses won't wear winter
            wool in warm weather.

What Got Caught

What got caught got canned,
What escaped, still swam!

Flipper Footsteps

Freely flapping flipper footsteps.
Freely flapping flipper footsteps.
Freely flapping flipper footsteps.

The Hobbled Filly

Clattering across the crooked cobblestones,
   the hobbled filly faltered home!
Clattering across the crooked cobblestones,
   the hobbled filly faltered home!
Clattering across the crooked cobblestones,
   the hobbled filly faltered home!

To Fool a Mule

If you'll fool a mule you'll feel a fool.
If you'll fool a mule you'll feel a fool.
If you'll fool a mule you'll feel a fool.

The Chameleon

Come here, complex chameleon!
Come here, complex chameleon!
Come here, complex chameleon!

Grumpy Bees

Grumpy bumble bees buzz by bumpy
    bumbleberries.
Grumpy bumble bees buzz by bumpy
    bumbleberries.
Grumpy bumble bees buzz by bumpy
    bumbleberries.

Bad Bumblebees
Bad bumblebee boo-boo.
Bad bumblebee boo-boo.
Bad bumblebee boo-boo.

Bees Knees

Bumble bees boast bumpy knees.
Bumble bees boast bumpy knees.
Bumble bees boast bumpy knees.

Keeping Cats Calm

Cat coats can't keep cats calm.
Cat coats can't keep cats calm.
Cat coats can't keep cats calm.

Mucky Ducks

Mucky ducks run amuck.
Mucky ducks run amuck.
Mucky ducks run amuck.

Watchdogs and Warthogs

Would a watch dog
   ward off a warthog?
If a warthog wanted,
   wouldn't the warthog
   hear the watch which
   the watchdog wore?

Too Much Smooch

The Duchess might just
   smooch her pooch too much!
The Duchess might just
   smooch her pooch too much!
The Duchess might just
   smooch her pooch too much!

Hippo Pillow

Puffy hippo pillow.
     Puffy hippo pillow.
          Puffy hippo pillow.

Slippery Sloth

A slippery sloth with snaily slime.
A slippery sloth with snaily slime.
A slippery sloth with snaily slime.

Sixty Snakes

Sixty slinky snakes singing silly songs.
Sixty slinky snakes singing silly songs.
Sixty slinky snakes singing silly songs.

Philippine Fishery
Famous Philippine fishery.
Famous Philippine fishery.
Famous Philippine fishery.

chapter 3

Emily's Enemies

A tongue twister by any other name...

This is where it gets personal! Name calling is
serious business and, if you're going to toss
twisters around with your friends, this is a good
place to start. When you get through with these,
take a look at the slovenly bunch you call pals and
start making up tongue twisters with their names.
That ought to keep you off the streets...

Emily's Enemies

Emily's enemies, unexpectedly eaten by envy,
  are eagerly eating eggs.
Emily's enemies, unexpectedly eaten by envy,
  are eagerly eating eggs.
Emily's enemies, unexpectedly eaten by envy,
  are eagerly eating eggs.

Dan's Can-Can

Dan can't Can-Can, can Don?
Dan can't Can-Can, can Don?
Dan can't Can-Can, can Don?

Sheila Shines Silver

Sheila shined her sister's silver.
Sheila shined her sister's silver.
Sheila shined her sister's silver.

Stella's Stamps

Stella stuck several sticky stamps.
Stella stuck several sticky stamps.
Stella stuck several sticky stamps.

Squeaky Shoes

Sue's shoes sure sound squeaky!
Sue's shoes sure sound squeaky!
Sue's shoes sure sound squeaky!

Shoddy Shoes

Shoddy, soggy shoes.
Shoddy, soggy shoes.
Shoddy, soggy shoes.

Spitball Pitfall

Fat Paul's pitfall was his spitball.
Fat Paul's pitfall was his spitball.
Fat Paul's pitfall was his spitball.

Louis and Louise

Louis let Louise leave last!
Louis let Louise leave last!
Louis let Louise leave last!

Pamela's Posies

Pamela's posies
  are supposed to be roses,
But she planted the posies
  so posies' what growses.

Frilly Phyllis

Frilly things fill Phyllis' filmy frock.
Frilly things fill Phyllis' filmy frock.
Frilly things fill Phyllis' filmy frock.

Another Zither

Is there another zither
  other than your sister's zither?
Is there another zither
  other than your sister's zither?
Is there another zither
  other than your sister's zither?

Patricia's Wishes

Patricia officially wishes for fish.
Patricia officially wishes for fish.
Patricia officially wishes for fish.

Tina's Toddler

Tina's toddler's too much trouble.
Tina's toddler's too much trouble.
Tina's toddler's too much trouble.

Heather's Feather Treasure

Did Heather ever wear the feather treasure in
  heady weather?
Did Heather ever wear the feather treasure in
  heady weather?
Did Heather ever wear the feather treasure in
  heady weather?

Hippo Hugs

Heavy-hearted hippo hugs.
Heavy-hearted hippo hugs.
Heavy-hearted hippo hugs.

Bubba's Bubbles

What's the trouble with the bubbles Bubba blew?
What's the trouble with the bubbles Bubba blew?
What's the trouble with the bubbles Bubba blew?

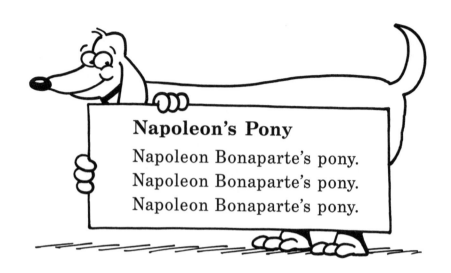

Napoleon's Pony

Napoleon Bonaparte's pony.
Napoleon Bonaparte's pony.
Napoleon Bonaparte's pony.

Handsome Hanson

Handsome Hanson
   ran some mansion,
   handed down from
   son to grandson.

Pooped Troops

Bernard Floop flogged his pooped troops.
Bernard Floop flogged his pooped troops.
Bernard Floop flogged his pooped troops.

Elephant Exercise

Ella Elephant exercises excessively.
Ella Elephant exercises excessively.
Ella Elephant exercises excessively.

Who Ron Wrote

Ron wrote the wrong one.
Ron wrote the wrong one.
Ron wrote the wrong one.

Similar Symbols

Several similar symbols.
Several similar symbols.
Several similar symbols.

Don's Dad

Don's dad didn't doubt Don didn't do the deed he
   said he didn't do;
   he doubted Don didn't do another deed
   Don did.

Chapter 4

Want a Way to Get a Waiter?

Eating and enunciating are bad company!

And now it's time to start the food fights. Face it, food is funny stuff. And it's even funnier when you get in there and start messing it around with tongue twisters. Take a shot at these puppies. It's a great way to spoil a perfectly good meal and work up an appetite at the same time!

Otter Eats

Ed the Otter eats easy-over omelets. Oscar Otter only eats oats.

Ed the Otter eats easy-over omelets. Oscar Otter only eats oats.

Ed the Otter eats easy-over omelets. Oscar Otter only eats oats.

Pineapple Popsicle

A pineapple popsicle? Possibly!
A pineapple popsicle? Possibly!
A pineapple popsicle? Possibly!

Bumble Crumble Pie

I'll have ample apple dapple bumble crumble pie.
I'll have ample apple dapple bumble crumble pie.
I'll have ample apple dapple bumble crumble pie.

Prying Pie

Why try to pry a pie apart?
Why not try to supply
    every guy a pumpkin pie or tart?

Kumquat Coating

Kumquat compote coating.
Kumquat compote coating.
Kumquat compote coating.

Bean Dreams

Baked beans bring bad dreams.
Baked beans bring bad dreams.
Baked beans bring bad dreams.

Susie's Applesauce

Susie's super applesauce
Susie's super applesauce
Susie's super applesauce

Peach Eating

Peach eating beats peach pitting!
Peach eating beats peach pitting.
Peach eating beats peach pitting.

Lizard Lunch

Lazy lizards love lunch.
Lazy lizards love lunch.
Lazy lizards love lunch.

Weary Waiter

What a way to wake a weary waiter!
What a way to wake a weary waiter!
What a way to wake a weary waiter!

Sipping Supper

Simply sipping supper slowly.
Simply sipping supper slowly.
Simply sipping supper slowly.

Sally's Soup

Sally sipped a saucer of simmering soup.
Sally sipped a saucer of simmering soup.
Sally sipped a saucer of simmering soup.

Whisk the Bisque

Want to whisk the bisque quicker
    or stir the stew?
Want to whisk the bisque quicker
    or stir the stew?
Want to whisk the bisque quicker
    or stir the stew?

Frank's Falafel

Awful Frank's falafel fell fully on the floor afore he
    was fully full.
Awful Frank's falafel fell fully on the floor afore he
    was fully full.
Awful Frank's falafel fell fully on the floor afore he
    was fully full.

Flying Fish

Flying fish fry.
Flying fish fry.
Flying fish fry.

Fresh Fish

Fresh fish flash fried.
Fresh fish flash fried.
Fresh fish flash fried.

Fish Stew

Fish stew simmers.
Fish stew simmers.
Fish stew simmers.

Treacherous Trevor

Treacherous Trevor tracked trout.
Treacherous Trevor tracked trout.
Treacherous Trevor tracked trout.

Sally's Salmon

Sally slapped a silly salmon.
Sally slapped a silly salmon.
Sally slapped a silly salmon.

Tabby's Tuna

Tabby tested ten tempting tins of tuna.
Tabby tested ten tempting tins of tuna.
Tabby tested ten tempting tins of tuna.

Flipping Flapjacks

Flipping frying flapjacks
fills Philip's Friday.
Flipping frying flapjacks
fills Philip's Friday.
Flipping frying flapjacks
fills Philip's Friday.

Baking Brown Bread

Barbara's brother's baking brown bread.
Barbara's brother's baking brown bread.
Barbara's brother's baking brown bread.

Pepper Powder

Peter properly prepares pepper powder.
Peter properly prepares pepper powder.
Peter properly prepares pepper powder.

Coughing Coffee

Cathy coughed coffee on Connie's copy.
Cathy coughed coffee on Connie's copy.
Cathy coughed coffee on Connie's copy.

Sweet Cinnamon

Sweet cinnamon sediment.
Sweet cinnamon sediment.
Sweet cinnamon sediment.

Mike and Ike

Ike likes ice like Mike likes rice!
Ike likes ice like Mike likes rice!
Ike likes ice like Mike likes rice!

Freaky Flies

Freaky flies frequently flee French fries.
Freaky flies frequently flee French fries.
Freaky flies frequently flee French fries.

Stinky Stilton

Silly Stanley sampled stinky Stilton.
Silly Stanley sampled stinky Stilton.
Silly Stanley sampled stinky Stilton.

Ten Toasts

Ten toasts for the tense host
Whose hens we tasted and roast we ate.
Ten toasts for the tense host
Whose hens we tasted and roast we ate.
Ten toasts for the tense host
Whose hens we tasted and roast we ate.

Elephant Olives

If all of the olives were elephant olives, one olive
    would almost feed all of us.
If all of the olives were elephant olives, one olive
    would almost feed all of us.
If all of the olives were elephant olives, one olive
    would almost feed all of us.

The Winner

The slimmer the dinner,
    the thinner the winner!

Chapter 5

Pesky Words

Tongue twisters only a mother could love!

Oh, it's not pretty, my friends. Here we get into the realm of the truly ridiculous, the stupifyingly silly, and the downright made up. Some of these are slightly nasty. Some are confounding. But they are all a little pesky when you get right down to it!

The Bore Next Door

The bore next door hexed our door,
   now we're vexed lest we snore!
The bore next door hexed our door,
   now we're vexed lest we snore!
The bore next door hexed our door,
   now we're vexed lest we snore!

Flaw Finder

If he finds a flaw, he'll flog the fool whose
   flaw he saw!
If he finds a flaw, he'll flog the fool whose
   flaw he saw!
If he finds a flaw, he'll flog the fool whose
   flaw he saw!

Sashed Assassin

An assassin in a sash.
An assassin in a sash.
An assassin in a sash.

Sorry She Spoke

Surely she was sorry she spoke so
    scandalously of Shirley!
Surely she was sorry she spoke so
    scandalously of Shirley!
Surely she was sorry she spoke so
    scandalously of Shirley!

Crooked Crickets

Crooked crickets kill crops.
Crooked crickets kill crops.
Crooked crickets kill crops.

Billy and Willy

As silly as Billy is,
He's better than Willy is,
As Willy is silly and bilious!

Trolls in Dungeons

Trolls toil in dungeons.
Trolls toil in dungeons.
Trolls toil in dungeons.

Proper Princesses

Perfectly proper princesses prepare pies.
Perfectly proper princesses prepare pies.
Perfectly proper princesses prepare pies.

Silly Shorts

Sherrie sports a silly sort of shorts.
Sherrie sports a silly sort of shorts.
Sherrie sports a silly sort of shorts.

Seeing What Arkansas

I saw the sight Arkansas.
I saw the sight Arkansas.
I saw the sight Arkansas.

Coffins Carry Off Coughers

Coffins often carry off
  the carrion of chaps who coughed.
Coffins often carry off
  the carrion of chaps who coughed.
Coffins often carry off
  the carrion of chaps who coughed.

Pests

A pessimist is, at best, a pest,
  And a cynic seldom lets you rest.
A pessimist is, at best, a pest,
  And a cynic seldom lets you rest.
A pessimist is, at best, a pest,
  And a cynic seldom lets you rest.

Chapter 6

Sounds Funny

Great out loud tongue twisters

Well, if you're doing anything right, by this time you've driven most of the people you know nuts with tongue twisters. But just to make sure, here are some extra great ones for those same people to try saying out loud. Make them spit and sputter and they'll love you forever. Or maybe not. But it will be fun to watch. And that's what really counts.

Peasant or Present?

Would you prefer a peasant pucker
or a pleasant present?
   Would you prefer a peasant pucker
   or a pleasant present?
      Would you prefer a peasant pucker
      or a pleasant present?

Stumped!

Simon's stumped. Send Stan a simpler sample.
Simon's stumped. Send Stan a simpler sample.
Simon's stumped. Send Stan a simpler sample.

The Crying Clown

The crying clown's cracked crown.
The crying clown's cracked crown.
The crying clown's cracked crown.

Showy Shoes

She shouldn't stow such showy shoes, should she?
She shouldn't stow such showy shoes, should she?
She shouldn't stow such showy shoes, should she?

Rich Witch

Which rich witch went every which way?
Which rich witch went every which way?
Which rich witch went every which way?

Poor Valerie

Valerie rarely ever varies.
Valerie rarely ever varies.
Valerie rarely ever varies.

Winding Twine

When you wind twine, mind your behind
   is not intertwined in the line that you wind.

Lollipops

A lollipop you lick a lot is not a lot of lollipop.
A lollipop you lick a lot is not a lot of lollipop.
A lollipop you lick a lot is not a lot of lollipop.

An Eerie Morning

An early eerie morning on a misty,
   moldy mooring.
An early eerie morning on a misty,
   moldy mooring.
An early eerie morning on a misty,
   moldy mooring.

A Stunning Jump

Certainly, a stunning jump
while cycling is a cunning stunt,
but so is seeing the jumper dumped!

Stitching Socks

I stitched a spot on a spotted sock
I'd spotted stitching slipping off
And so I stitched the spot away
Upon the spotted spot upon the stocking
    spot today.

Which Was Worthier?

Which was worthier–the worrier, the wanderer,
    or the warrior?
Which was worthier–the worrier, the wanderer,
    or the warrior?
Which was worthier–the worrier, the wanderer,
    or the warrior?

A Matinee

A matinee movie viewed at midday
    is a marvelous method of missing a day!
A matinee movie viewed at midday
    is a marvelous method of missing a day!
A matinee movie viewed at midday
    is a marvelous method of missing a day!

Chapter 7

Short but Sweet

One line, one twisted tongue!

There's a great line that says "brevity is the soul of wit," which is a fancy way of saying shorter is funnier. Which is funny because it actually takes me a little while to explain what that means. Which isn't funny. And is too long. Oh, forget it! Read these. They're nice and short.

The Magician

Suspicious magician.
Suspicious magician.
Suspicious magician.

Dentist's Apprentice

The menacing dentist's apprentice.
The menacing dentist's apprentice.
The menacing dentist's apprentice.

Apostrophes

Preposterous apostrophes.
Preposterous apostrophes.
Preposterous apostrophes.

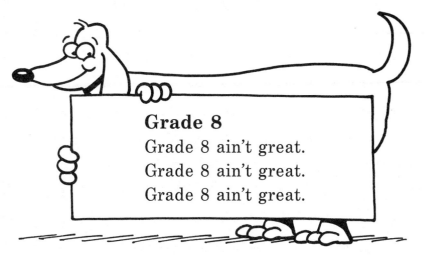

Grade 8

Grade 8 ain't great.
Grade 8 ain't great.
Grade 8 ain't great.

Thaw Those Toes

Thaw those three frozen toes.
Thaw those three frozen toes.
Thaw those three frozen toes.

Cock a Doodle

Cock a doodle do you do,
   cockatoo to meet you too!
Cock a doodle do you do,
   cockatoo to meet you too!
Cock a doodle do you do,
   cockatoo to meet you too!

Cockatoo

A cockatoo can keep a tune.
Can tuna fish too swoon the moon?

The Cow and the Crow

The cow cried moo, but the crow cawed true.
The cow cried moo, but the crow cawed true.
The cow cried moo, but the crow cawed true.

Sloppy Spooks

Sixty-six sloppy spooks.
Sixty-six sloppy spooks.
Sixty-six sloppy spooks.

Do You Stoop?

Do you stoop to sleuth or scent the scoop?
Do you stoop to sleuth or scent the scoop?
Do you stoop to sleuth or scent the scoop?

When Ben Bullied Brad

When Ben bullied Brad, Brad bullied Ben back.
When Ben bullied Brad, Brad bullied Ben back.
When Ben bullied Brad, Brad bullied Ben back.

Who Won?

Someone won some sum, son!
Someone won some sum, son!
Someone won some sum, son!

We Won!

We won when we wore our armor!
We won when we wore our armor!
We won when we wore our armor!

Watching the Walrus

We watched the walrus washing.
We watched the walrus washing.
We watched the walrus washing.

Sloppy Screens

Sloppy screens shield shabby shows.
Sloppy screens shield shabby shows.
Sloppy screens shield shabby shows.

Missing Mittens

The myth of the missing mittens.
The myth of the missing mittens.
The myth of the missing mittens.

Winter's White

Winter's all white, all right.
Winter's all white, all right.
Winter's all white, all right.

Sled, Shed, and Lettuce

If a sled is red and a shed is red, is a shredded
head of lettuce red?
If a sled is red and a shed is red, is a shredded
head of lettuce red?
If a sled is red and a shed is red, is a shredded
head of lettuce red?

Sore Tooth

Forsooth, sore tooth!
Forsooth, sore tooth!
Forsooth, sore tooth!

The Book Box

The book box looks locked!
The book box looks locked!
The book box looks locked!

Shame About Shortages

Such a shame to see such shortages!
Such a shame to see such shortages!
Such a shame to see such shortages!

Slick Suits

Slick suits sure suit Sven!
Slick suits sure suit Sven!
Slick suits sure suit Sven!

Simple and Stylish

Sport something simple and stylish.
Sport something simple and stylish.
Sport something simple and stylish.

Find the Filthy Outlaw!

Find the fifth filthy outlaw!
Find the fifth filthy outlaw!
Find the fifth filthy outlaw!

Walking West

When walking west, one rarely wanders.
When walking west, one rarely wanders.
When walking west, one rarely wanders.

Show Up at Sixish

So, should we show up say at sixish?
So, should we show up say at sixish?
So, should we show up say at sixish?

Sock Shops

If sock shops sold stocks, sock stocks
could be hot stocks.

Blue Buggies

Bright blue buggies
Bright blue buggies
Bright blue buggies

Chapter 8

Sputtering Sports

Take a crack at these curveballs!

Here's your chance to show that you truly are a sport! Keep your eye on the ball and see what you can do with these. And remember, if you don't see your favorite game on the following pages, that means it's your turn to invent some new tongue twisters. Batter up!

Foul Ball!

Can't a fly ball be called a foul
  by the fellow who finds fouls
  without the frothing fans finding fault
  with his finding of the foul?

Steee-rike!

If you're pitching, itching each
and every inning isn't actually
that fetching!

Hooper's Hopes

Hooper hoped he'd hit a homer, but Hooper hit
his hurt hand.

Hooper hoped he'd hit a homer, but Hooper hit
his hurt hand.

Hooper hoped he'd hit a homer, but Hooper hit
his hurt hand.

What Pros Prefer

Pros prefer proper putters.
Pros prefer proper putters.
Pros prefer proper putters.

What Pros Peel

Pro players peel pale pears.
Pro players peel pale pears.
Pro players peel pale pears.

Surfer Summons

Summer summons some surfers!
Summer summons some surfers!
Summer summons some surfers!

The Wreck

The wreck they wreaked
   wasn't worked on a wrecking rock,
   but was weakly washed
   by leaking water wicking in.

Alan Angled

Alan angled expertly.
Alan angled expertly.
Alan angled expertly.

Seven Sailboats

Seven sailboats steered with sextants.
Seven sailboats steered with sextants.
Seven sailboats steered with sextants.

Way to Go

What way were we when we went way wrong?
What way were we when we went way wrong?
What way were we when we went way wrong?

Tim and Jim

The twins, Tim and Jim,
  will wish to win the race they're in!
The twins, Tim and Jim,
  will wish to win the race they're in!
The twins, Tim and Jim,
  will wish to win the race they're in!

What Did They Throw?

They threw the thing they think they threw.
They threw the thing they think they threw.
They threw the thing they think they threw.

The Game

Say, what a shame the game's a sham.
Say, what a shame the game's a sham.
Say, what a shame the game's a sham.

Going for Gold

Gordie the goalie gladly going for gold.
Gordie the goalie gladly going for gold.
Gordie the goalie gladly going for gold.

Soccer Shorts

Silken satin sequined soccer shorts.
Silken satin sequined soccer shorts.
Silken satin sequined soccer shorts.

Hockey Stick

A hockey stick is not
a stocking gift.
  A hockey stick is not
  a stocking gift.
    A hockey stick is not
    a stocking gift.

The Slap Shot Slipped Past

The slap shot slipped past so fast it shot past a
slipshod stuck out stick.
  The slap shot slipped past so fast it shot past a
  slipshod stuck out stick.
    The slap shot slipped past so fast it shot
    past a slipshod stuck out stick.

Chapter 9

The Kitchen Sink

This is where we pull out all the stops!

All right, this is where we throw the book at them! Well, don't actually throw this book, you could put someone's eye out! Just let them have it with the tongue twisters that follow. By now, you'll be able to whiz through these with no problems!

Vocal Classes

Why buy vocal classes and not bi-focal glasses?
Why buy vocal classes and not bi-focal glasses?
Why buy vocal classes and not bi-focal glasses?

Silken Candles

Can't sell silken candles.
Can't sell silken candles.
Can't sell silken candles.

Skim Some

Skim some, sling some, ship some, keep some.
Skim some, sling some, ship some, keep some.
Skim some, sling some, ship some, keep some.

Time Trample

I ought to
talk to the shop
about the tocking
of the clock
and the stalling
in the gearing
and the squeaking
sound I'm hearing
and the sticking of the ticking
of the small hand of my watch.

Breathe Deeply

Rest your wits,
Arrest your wrist,
Your watch is not
Abreast of which
Or why or who or even how,
So wrest your wrist watch
From your brow.
The when will wait a little now.

A Swift Push

She wished her sister pushed us swifter.
She wished her sister pushed us swifter.
She wished her sister pushed us swifter.

Sure, She's Shy

Sure, she's shy, so she stays inside.
Sure, she's shy, so she stays inside.
Sure, she's shy, so she stays inside.

She Quit Court

She quit court quite quietly
And quickly too!
  She quit court quite quietly
  And quickly too!
    She quit court quite quietly
    And quickly too!

Stunned Stan

Stunned, Stan stood stock still.
Stunned, Stan stood stock still.
Stunned, Stan stood stock still.

Sawing Suzy's Seesaw

Saw you sawing Suzy's seesaw!
Saw you sawing Suzy's seesaw!
Saw you sawing Suzy's seesaw!

Pick a Spot

Pick a special spot to picnic.
Pick a special spot to picnic.
Pick a special spot to picnic.

In the Pasture

Perfect your posture in the pasture.
Perfect your posture in the pasture.
Perfect your posture in the pasture.

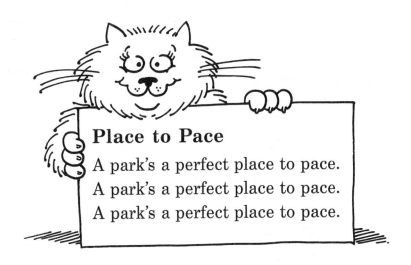

Place to Pace

A park's a perfect place to pace.
A park's a perfect place to pace.
A park's a perfect place to pace.

The Bouncer and the Pouncer

One waits and bounces
while the other
waits to pounce
and ounce by ounce
and inch by inch
the one that waits
will all at once
pounce upon the bouncer!

We'll Wheel Right

We'll wheel right when the wheelwright rears.
We'll wheel right when the wheelwright rears.
We'll wheel right when the wheelwright rears.

Watch the Wheel Rut

Watch the wheel rut in the road.
Watch the wheel rut in the road.
Watch the wheel rut in the road.

A Twisted Wrist

A twisted wrist arrested is a casted, plastered,
wrested wrist.
A twisted wrist arrested is a casted, plastered,
wrested wrist.
A twisted wrist arrested is a casted, plastered,
wrested wrist.

Tongue Twister Tag

A twisted tongue tied,
tortures some,
until the twisted tongue is fun,
At which point
twisted tongues insist
To try the trick out
and persist
To twist the tongue
if not the wrist
Of all untwisted tongues
they've missed!

INDEX